rabbits

understanding and
caring for your pet

Written by
Dr Anne McBride BSc PhD Cert.Cons FRSA

rabbits

understanding and
caring for your pet

Written by
Dr Anne McBride BSc PhD Cert.Cons FRSA

Magnet & Steel Ltd

www.magnetsteel.com

Printed by Printworks Global Ltd. London/Hong Kong

ISBN: 978-1-907337-05-5
ISBN: 1-907337-05-9

Contents

Perfect pets

The rabbit is a firm favourite with families all over the world. Apart from cats and dogs it is the most popular of all the furry (mammal) creatures we keep as pets.

There are many reasons for its huge popularity:

- Rabbits, if treated gently, are friendly animals and like to be petted by their owners.

- Rabbits are not expensive to buy, and once you have bought your initial equipment, they are relatively inexpensive to keep, compared to a cat or dog.

- However, be aware that appropriate accommodation will be quite expensive and costs of feed and veterinary fees, such as for vaccinations and neutering must be factored into your decision to obtain rabbits as pets.

- Rabbits are hardy animals that can live in outside accommodation of a hutch and run, so long as the hutch is kept warm and draft free.

- Rabbits can also live in the house, in a suitably sized cage and attached exercise area, and can spend some time roaming free in other safe areas of the house.

- Rabbits are most active in the early morning and in the evening, whereas some small animals, such as hamsters, are active at night.

- Rabbits come in many different colours, sizes and coat types so you can choose your favourite.

Special requirements

Rabbits are among the most appealing of all small animals kept as pets, with their large eyes, big ears, and quiet habits.
But, like all animals, they have their own specific needs which you need to know about before buying your first rabbit.
This is important so you can have a good relationship with your rabbits, and they can live long, healthy and happy lives.

- You will need to handle your rabbits gently, as they are easily frightened, especially when picked up. For this reason, they are not good pets for children under the age of seven.

- You need to give your rabbits the right food to stay fit and healthy.

- You will need to frequently clean out the rabbits' home.

- You need to provide a large, safe area where your rabbits can exercise every day outside its hutch or cage.

- You will need to make arrangements for someone to look after your rabbits if you go away on holiday.

- You will need to take your rabbits to the vet regularly, once or twice a year for vaccination against Myxomatosis and VHD. These illnesses can kill rabbits, even if the rabbits are kept indoors.

- You will need to regularly, weekly, check the rabbits' teeth and nails to ensure they are not overgrown.

- You will need to be able to keep two rabbits together for companionship and commit to looking after your rabbits throughout their lives, which may be 10 years.

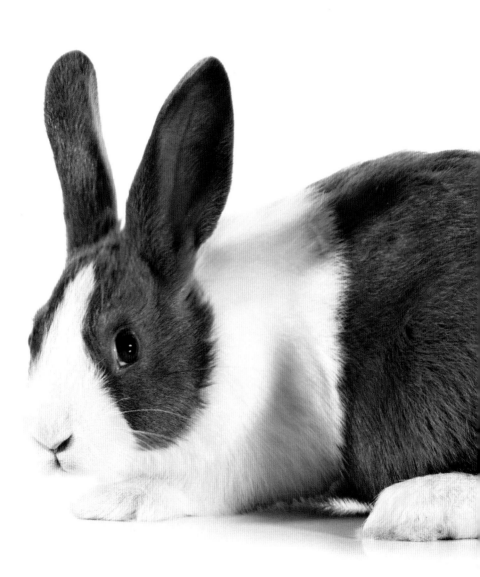

Rabbit history

The ancestors of all our pet rabbits originally came from Spain and Portugal. Fossil remains of rabbits date back over 4,000 years.

Known as the European rabbit, it is one of the most successful of all small animals and is famous for being able to quickly populate an area. This is because their needs are simple. So long as they have plenty of grass (hay) and plants to eat, and ground in which they can dig a warm, safe home, wild rabbits can live and breed almost anywhere.

The biggest danger that rabbits face is from meat-eating hunters, and all rabbits are continuously on the lookout for danger. But rabbits have found that safety lies in numbers. If there are a lot of rabbits living together, they can warn each other of danger, and they will be harder to catch. If a hunter approaches, the alarm signal is given by a rabbit thumping the ground with its hind legs, and the rabbits run to the safety of their underground home.

Warren life

Rabbits live in family groups in a rambling underground home called a warren. There are many entrances and exits, sleeping areas and even nursery runs for litters of baby rabbits (kits).

Rabbits are active animals and wild rabbits will travel the length of 30 tennis courts every day as they eat grass and socialise with their friends. This natural behaviour needs to be considered when providing accommodation for pet rabbits. They need shelter, and to be able to run, jump, dig and forage every day.

If a female rabbit (doe) is expecting young, she will make a nest using hair from her underbelly. The babies are born without fur, their eyes are closed and they cannot hear. But they develop very quickly. Within two months they no longer need to be cared for by their mother, and within four months the young rabbits are ready to breed.

Wild rabbits have their babies in the spring and summer, and they have several litters a year. On average, there are five kits in a litter, so a single female may have 30 babies in a year, and may even be a grandmother by autumn. So, the numbers of rabbits can grow at a great rate.

Spot the difference

Hares and rabbits both belong to the Lagomorph family, and look very alike. They eat the same food, and they are both hunted by larger meat-eating predators. But the hare and the rabbit have found different ways to survive in the wild.

The rabbit escapes its enemies by fleeing underground. The hare lives above ground and relies on its speed. Hares have longer legs than rabbits, which means they can run faster. If a hare is being chased it can reach a speed of 45 miles per hour to out-run its enemy.

Baby hares (leverets) are born fully furred with eyes open, ready to run. Baby rabbits are born blind and without fur.

To find out more about rabbits, and hares, see the suggested further reading at the end of this book.

Top: Hare
Bottom: Rabbit

The human link

People soon caught on to the idea that rabbits could provide a tasty meal. Man has hunted wild rabbits since earliest times. But the Romans realised that it was easier to keep rabbits rather than go out and hunt them. In the first century AD they constructed walled enclosures for rabbits, called Leporaria. Rabbits were bred for their meat and also for their fur. In fact, rabbits were so highly valued that an image of a rabbit was put on coins during the reign of Emperor Hadrian in the years 120-130 AD.

Going global

Following the Roman example, the Normans also kept rabbits. When they conquered Britain in 1066, they brought rabbits with them. The Normans constructed special rabbit gardens. The rabbits were confined in a field where they dug a warren. The field was surrounded by a deep ditch and a high bank to stop rabbits escaping. But rabbits found it easy to dig their way out, and in no time they had spread far and wide.

When the first European settlers were making their homes in the United States and in Australia, the rabbit went along too. Rabbits have been so successful in the wild that they now live in every continent on earth, except Antarctica.

But wild rabbits feast on crops of wheat, vegetables and lettuces which is food grown by farmers for us. Three rabbits can eat as much grass in a day as one sheep, so a large number of rabbits can do terrible damage to a farm, and rabbits are a major menace to agriculture. In many countries there are continuing attempts to control the numbers of wild rabbits.

Pet rabbits

By the 1800s, many people, particularly poorer people, kept rabbits as a source of meat for the table and from this grew the fashion for keeping and breeding the prettier ones. So by the mid-19th century people had also started keeping rabbits for showing and as pets.

Some people are allergic to the fur of animals, and may suffer health problems if a pet is kept in the house. Your doctor can test for this, and if you have a problem, you may still be able to keep your rabbits outside in a hutch with a run attached and enjoy watching them.

The rabbit's world

Find out how a rabbit functions and how it sees the world.

Nose

The constantly twitching nose shows how important the rabbit's sense of smell is. The rabbit relies on smell to find the best food, to avoid poisonous plants, and to detect the scent of a nearby predator.

Whiskers

The whiskers are used for touch, to measure the width of tunnels, and to help the rabbit find its way in the dark.

Mouth

The rabbit has a large tongue and a sensitive upper lip, which it uses to test if items can be eaten.

Teeth

The rabbit's 28 teeth grow all the time – up to 12.5 cm (5 inches) in a year. This is why a constant supply of good quality hay is essential to prevent dental problems. Rabbit teeth are specially designed to slice and grind grass and hay, the rabbit's natural food.

Eyes

Rabbits can see behind them and to the sides, and above but not right in front of the nose. They have excellent distance vision for movement, to help them detect predators, but they are colour blind.

Front legs

They are strong and short, and are used for digging.

Hind legs

The hind legs are longer than the front legs. They are very powerful and are used for kicking away earth when a rabbit is digging.

Feet

The soles of the feet have a covering of fur which provides a firm grip on all kinds of surfaces.

Movement

The longer hind legs give the rabbit its hopping gait, and enables it to move very fast, leaping and twisting to avoid predators. When investigating a new area, rabbits will move quite slowly and timidly using a slow, awkward looking walking movement.

Tail

This is known as the 'scut'. It is short and upturned, usually showing pale hair on the underside. Bucks (males) carry their tails high when defending their territory or courting does (females). Both bucks and does lift their tails high to show the pale underside when they are running away from something frightening.

Body

The body is generally compact and lightweight, although this does depend on the breed.

Coat

The coat may be short-haired or long-haired, or even curly. It may feel like velvet or like satin.

Ears

Wild rabbits and many breeds of domestic rabbits have upright ears. Each ear can act on its own, and can be swivelled around so that the rabbit can tune into sound coming from any direction. The ears on Lop-eared breeds flop down alongside the head, and these rabbits may not hear quite as well and are certainly more prone to developing ear problems.

Colours & markings

Rabbits come in a wide range of colours and markings. Many are self-explanatory, but the list below will help you understand a selection of the more common terms:

Agouti

Like a wild rabbit, with more than one colour on each strand, usually grey and brown. Blue: an even blue grey. Broken marked: like 'Butterfly' (below), but more varied markings on predominantly white fur.

Butterfly

White with a butterfly-shaped colour marking on the nose. Coloured ears and patches around the eyes, a large coloured patch on the back and variable amounts of spotting.

Chocolate

Deep brown with light grey undercoat.

Chinchilla

Almost silver, like a chinchilla.

Fawn

Deep golden colour on back, flanks and chest. White eye circles, inner ear, chin, belly and tail.

Lilac

Pinky dove grey.

Otter

Black, blue, chocolate or lilac coloured with a creamy white belly that blends to tan coloured edges.

Sealpoint/ Siamese

Like Siamese cats, a beige-grey body colour that fades into a darker coloured face, ears, paws and tail.

Tortoiseshell/ Sooty fawn

Also called 'Madagascar'. Orangey brown top coat
with a blue undercoat. Sides, face, ears, legs, feet and
tail are dark grey.

Steel

Similar to chinchilla, but darker.

Brindle pattern

Mix of two colours, one light and one dark,
consistently across the body.

Broken pattern

Bi-colour or Tri-colour.

Marked pattern

Usually white with one other coloured pattern all over.

Self pattern

One solid colour.

Tan pattern

Solid colour head, back, sides, outer ear, front foreleg,
back legs and top of tail. Lighter eye circles, chest
and underside.

Ticked pattern

Majority base colour with contrasting solid or tipped
guard hairs.

Rabbit breeds

Pet rabbits come in a variety of breeds as well as colours. The weight of a rabbit varies according to breed and can range from 2 lb (900 g) to 20 lb (9 kg).

The first pet rabbits looked just like the European Wild Rabbit. They were small, brownish-coloured animals with short hair.

It did not take people long to realise that they could create more exotic-looking rabbits. Now you can have rabbits of different sizes, with different types of ears, all in a dazzling array of colours, with different coat types and textures. This variety has in no small way contributed in establishing their popularity amongst enthusiasts and pet keepers.

The breeds are normally divided into Lop, Fancy, Fur and Rex rabbits. Choosing the right one for you is down to preference, experience and availability.

Many of the rabbits you find in your local pet store will be crossbreeds, which make great pets, but these are some of the more common breeds you may find. If you are wanting a particular breed which is not available at your pet store, you could try your local rabbit rescue, or contact The British Rabbit Council or American Rabbit Breeders Association to find your nearest reputable breeder.

Please note that the rabbits shown in the breed section are not perfect 'breed standard' examples. They are pet rabbits, more like those available from pet stores. For accurate breed standard, visit the websites of The British Rabbit Council or American Rabbit Breeders Association.

If you want pet rabbits for a child, it is better to buy medium or large breeds, which will weigh 6 lb (3 kg) or more when adult. These tend to be more placid and, being too big for the child to pick up, are less likely to be frightened or accidentally injured. Many rabbits end up being given away to rescue because they have become frightened when being picked up and have learnt to nip and kick people who try to lift them. The larger breeds include the English, New Zealand, Californian Gigantica, Flemish and British giants and French lop.

Remember all rabbits if not frightened, given plenty of space to exercise and play and the right food will be good natured and inquisitive animals.

English

Size:	5.9- 7.9 lb (2.7- 3.6 kg) Medium
Colour:	Black, blue, tortoiseshell, chocolate or grey.
Lifespan:	8- 10 years

The English is one of the oldest breeds, dating back to the first half of the nineteenth century. They are attractively marked, often with a butterfly marking around the nose and mouth area.

Besides the five colours recognised for showing, other markings commonly appear and are no less attractive for a pet. When English rabbits are bred together, it is common for some of the litter to be marked (spotted), some self-coloured (solid colouring all over) and the remainder will be Charlies, which are white, with coloured head markings, only a few spots and a stripe along the back.

Dutch

Size:	4.4- 5 lb (2- 2.2 kg) Small
Colour:	Black, blue, chocolate, yellow, tortoiseshell, grey.
Lifespan:	7- 10 years

The Dutch rabbit is a beautiful creature, characterised by a bright white inverted 'V' marking along the bridge of the nose, white band around the torso and white paws. The rest of the body can be a range of colours including black, blue, chocolate, yellow, tortoiseshell and grey (for showing) and several others, including tri-colour, are also seen. The coat is quite short and should be glossy.

Tan

Size:	4.4 lb (2 kg) Small
Colour:	Black and tan, black, blue, chocolate and tan.
Lifespan:	5- 8 years

The standard colouration of the Tan is similar to that of a Doberman dog, although the two are rarely compared!

The breed dates back to the 1880's, but the origin of the first 'Black and Tan' is still something of a mystery, most likely the crossing of wild and Dutch rabbits. Various crossings have created other colour combinations since then.

Most commonly found with a black body, with tan underside, eye circles, ears, nose and tail. It has a solid, rounded body.

Angora

Size: 5.8- 7.8 lb (2.5- 3.4 kg) Medium
Colour: Wide range of colours.
Lifespan: 5- 8 years

The Angora is undoubtedly one of the oldest breeds of rabbit. There are numerous accounts of its origins, from stories that it came from the Angora province of Turkey, to being named the Angora because of the resemblance of the coat to the Angora Goat. Several others claim that the Angora's history is exclusively English. What is certain, is that the breed is popular across the globe, with many breeds of Angora now recognised.

Most Angoras are white albinos, but there are many colour groups, including self, agouti and shaded. The coat of the Angora is more accurately described as wool, which can grow to around 10 cm in length.

The coat requires a great deal of care, so Angoras should only be considered as a pet if you have the time, patience and knowledge to care for one.

Himalayan

Size: 4.4 lb (2 kg) Small
Colour: White with black, chocolate, blue or lilac points on paws, nose and ears. Pink eyes.
Life: 5- 8 years

The Himalayan is a very old breed and is in fact one of the original colour variants to be created as a food stock breed in Asia. This small, slim rabbit has quite distinctive markings. The breed is classified as cylindrical, as they have long tube-like bodies (they are even judged at shows in a stretched out position). The coat is mainly white, but the ears, nose (and face), tail and feet are coloured with black, blue, chocolate or lilac. They are born white with markings that develop with age. They have red/pink eyes.

Notice how their long bodies differ to most of the more rounded rabbit breeds.

Chinchilla

Size:	4.4- 12.1 lb (2- 5.5 kg) Standard— Giganta
Colour:	Silver with white & black fleck.
Lifespan:	4- 7 years

The Chinchilla comes in two sizes: Standard 2- 3 kg (Small) and the Giganta (Large) weighing up to an impressive 5.5 kg.

In body shape and coat these rabbits are almost identical with the exception of only a small variation in body structure. It, unsurprisingly, resembles the Chinchilla in colour.

The Standard Chinchilla rabbit is French in origin while the Giganta is American and thought to be a closer bred specimen of the Flemish Giant and American Chinchilla rabbit, the giant being bred for both fur and meat. Body shape however, is very similar, with the standard showing a slightly arched back compared to the giant, which has a slightly straighter spine and delicately lighter coat.

Silver Fox

Colours:	Black, blue, chocolate & lilac
Weight:	5.5- 7 lb (2.5- 3.2 kg) Medium
Lifespan:	7- 9 years

The silver fox is best known for its beautiful dense and silky fur. The glossy coat will need regular brushing to keep it in a healthy condition.

It has a white belly with white ticking on the chest, flanks and feet. Its eye circles, inside of ears, nostrils and underside of jaw are also white. It has a broad head and solid body.

Lionhead

Colours: Various colours and patterns
Weight: 3- 3.75 lb (1.36- 1.7 kg) Small
Lifespan   8- 10 years

The lionhead gets its name from its lion like mane which forms a full circle around the head and falls into a fringe between the ears. However, not all lionheads keep a full mane as they grow older.

It is only a recent addition to England, being imported to the country in 1995. Since then its popularity has gone from strength to strength. Like the Angora, the Lionhead needs more frequent grooming than other breeds to keep the mane free of hay and bedding material. As a baby they need more brushing until they get their adult coat which is less woolly.

New Zealand

Size: 7.9- 11 lb (3.6- 5 kg) Medium
Colours: Red, white, black and blue.
Lifespan: 5- 8 years

The New Zealand rabbit can be found in red, white and less commonly, blue and black fur colourations. The red has a rich golden red colour that runs right down to the base of the fur, which has quite a coarse feel to it.

Although named the New Zealand, this breed was actually developed in the United States in the early 1900s as a meat and fur rabbit, but soon became popular as a pet.

The ears of a New Zealand rabbit stand upright and have thinner fur covering that allows their skin to show through.

Whites, blues and blacks are usually calmer than reds.

English Lop

Size: 7- 11 lb (3.2- 5 kg) Medium
Colour: Available in broken & solid
           patterns of various colours.
Lifespan: 5- 8 years

The impressive English Lop possesses perhaps the largest ears to body proportion in the animal world with ears that can measure an astonishing 70 cm (28 inches) in length from ear tip to ear tip and more than 18 cm (7 inches) in width.

They also have slighter shoulders to rump proportions, drawing further attention to the ears. It has a rather slender body, but is still robust like other lop breeds. It also has a pleasantly sloped forehead unlike the roman profile of the European/ Continental Lop breeds.

As the name suggest, the English Lop was developed in England in the early 1800s, although newer research suggests that the breed originated in Africa.

Special care needs to be taken of the ears, so this unusual breed is not usually recommended as a pet.

French Lop

Size:	9.9- 12.1 lb + (4.5- 5.5 kg +) Medium/ Large
Colour:	Available in solid and butterfly patterns of various colours.
Lifespan:	5- 8 years

The French Lop can weigh well over 5 kg. The breed was created by a Frenchman (M Cordonnier) in the middle of the nineteenth century, by crossing the English Lop with a giant European breed. It was originally bred for meat, but has become popular around the world as a pet.

The French Lop has much shorter ears than the English, however as with all the lop-eared breeds special care needs to be taken with the ears. They should extend to around 3- 4 cm below the jaw. It has a large, solid body that is well balanced and the ears hang and create a horseshoe-like shape around the head.

Harlequin

Size: Average 5.9- 7.9 lb (2.7- 3.6 kg)
Small
Colour: Two coloured with orange or
white & black/ brown/ blue/
lilac.
Life: 4- 8 years

The breed is divided into two colours types: Harlequin and Magpie. Their variations are the same, except the Magpie has white with a second colour. The face is split vertically between the two colours. Originally developed in France, the Harlequin has a dense, silky coat.

The Harlequin is a difficult rabbit to breed well, so it is no surprise that they are not seen as often as other breeds.

Rex

Size: 5.9- 7.9 lb (2.7- 3.6 kg)
        Standard (Medium)
        3.1- 4.8 lb (1.7- 2 kg) Mini (Small)
Colour: Wide range of colours & patterns.
Lifespan: 5- 8 years

Rex rabbits originated in France in the early 1900s from a mutation of mainly common rabbits. Both Standard and mini Rex are found in a vast array of colours, patterns and several coat types. The colours and markings include:

• Self - Black, Blue, Havana and Lilac

• Shaded - Sable Siamese and Smoke Pearl

• Tan pattern - Sable Marten and Otter

• Agouti pattern - Chinchilla and Opal

The Rex also has a number of coat types including the rare Astrex and Opossum. The standard coat is very velvety, which was prized by fur traders in the past. Its texture means that the Rex needs extra bedding for warmth and comfort. Rex (and Mini Rex) are very popular as show rabbits.

What type of rabbit do I want?

It is important to consider what type of rabbit you want, and to consider if you have the space to give them a proper home.

The next section gives an idea of things you need to consider before getting your pet rabbits.

Remember larger breeds are more suitable for children.

One rabbit or two?

Rabbits are social animals and it is strongly recommended that you have two, so that when you are not able to spend time with them, they will not be lonely. This need to provide our rabbits with suitable company is recognized in the animal welfare act as part of our responsibility for caring for them.

The best arrangement is to have a neutered male and neutered female. Rabbits can be neutered at around 3-4 months of age. Neutering will mean that you will not have unexpected baby rabbits which you may not be able to find good homes for. Neutering also helps prevent behaviour problems, such as fighting between rabbits of the same sex; spraying urine, which is part of courtship behaviour or pulling fur which is part of nesting behaviour and can be triggered by false as well as true pregnancy.

Two neutered males, who have known each
other since a few weeks old, can also live happily
together. However, if not neutered they are likely to
fight when adult.

It is not recommended to have two females as,
when adult, they may fight, even if they have
been neutered.

If you currently only have one rabbit, you may wish
to consider getting it a friend (of the opposite sex,
neutered). However, if it has lived on its own for
a long time it may not welcome another rabbit. In
that case, you must make sure your rabbit gets
plenty of attention from you, every day. You may
also wish to contact a good, reputable
rabbit rescue to see if they
will be able to help find
your rabbit a friend
and introduce them
appropriately.

RISEHOLME CAMPUS

Setting up home

Before you buy a rabbit, you will need to decide where you are going to keep it, and then buy suitable housing.

Whether you keep them outside or in your home, the rabbits' accommodation must have both a hutch (safe sleeping area) and a permanently attached exercise area (run) that it can access when it wants to. You may also want to have an additional run that you can move around the garden or safe areas where they can go free in your home (see page 76).

The great outdoors

Rabbits can live in an outside hutch-and-run complex all-year-round, as long as you take steps to make it as comfortable as possible for them.

- As an absolute minimum, the hutch should allow your rabbit to take three hops when it is fully grown. It is recommended that the minimum size is 6 feet x 2 feet x 2 feet high (1.8 m x 61 cm x 61 cm high) for a small, mini, breed of rabbit. Larger breeds require a significantly larger hutch.

- The hutch should be raised off the ground to prevent dampness and draughts.

- The hutch should have a separate sleeping compartment, with a cosy bed of hay and straw. The rest of the hutch should be lined with wood shavings, which help to absorb the rabbit's urine.

- The living quarters should have a fine, wire-mesh front, to stop rats or mice getting in.

- Both the hutch and the run must be made secure to protect the rabbit from larger enemies such as cats and foxes.

- A water bottle for small animals and a hay rack should be fitted to the side of the hutch.

In the winter, a hutch cover should be used, these can be bought or you can use some heavy sacking to reduce heat escaping from the roof of the hutch. This will provide extra protection from the cold. The cover can be pulled down to cover the front of the hutch at night, whist still allowing sufficient fresh air. In cold weather, do ensure the rabbit's water has not frozen, wrapping the bottle will help protect it from freezing. Your rabbit needs to be able to have fresh drinking water at all times.

Outside run

Rabbits kept in a hutch do not have very much room to move around, so they need a place where they can stretch their legs. Ideally the run should be permanently attached to the hutch so the rabbits can have free access to it and choose to go out when they want to. If the run is not permanently attached you will need to put your rabbits in it. Make sure there is a shelter, a dry, hay-filled area, raised off the ground and out of the rain and wind. Your rabbits should be given the opportunity to exercise for 6-8 hours a day.

- The run should be as big as possible, with a shaded area at one end here the rabbits can go if it gets too hot, or if it starts to rain.

- Attach a water-bottle to the side of run. You can also provide a selection of vegetables for your rabbits to eat, and toys such as branches of (untreated) fruit trees that they can strip the bark from. If the run is on grass, remember to keep moving the run so your rabbits have fresh grass to eat.

  If the run is on concrete, provide an area filled with sand / soil which will provide a soft resting place – a small sand pit is very suitable.

- The run should also contain things for your rabbit to use, and to help it feel safe, such as logs to sit on and use as look-out places, and half pipes to run through or hide in, should a large bird fly over, for example.

House rabbits

Keeping rabbits as house pets started in the USA in the 1980s, and now many owners prefer this way. House rabbits need a cage to use as a base.

- The indoor cage should be as big as possible. You can buy specially-made rabbit cages, or you can adapt a dog crate.

- The cage needs a shallow tray as a base which can be lined with newspaper, or you can use easy-to-clean carpet tiles.

- Rabbits will use a cat litter tray, and this should be placed in a corner of the cage. Line the cat litter tray with a 2.5 cm (1 inch) of litter, and then add a layer of hay, which will encourage your rabbits to use it.

- You can use washable fleece bedding for a comfortable bed.

- Attach a water bottle to the side of the cage.

Bunny-proofing your home

You can use a large playpen so that your rabbits can exercise outside their cage.

Many house rabbit owners 'bunny proof' a room, where the rabbits can hop around in safety. If you let your rabbits go free, watch out for the following hazards:

- Trailing electric wires.

- Floor-length curtains that are likely to be chewed.

- Houseplants will be seen as a tasty snack and are often poisonous to rabbits.

- Wallpaper shredding is a house rabbit speciality, so confine your rabbit to rooms with painted walls.

Do supervise your rabbits, especially if you have dogs or cats, or ferrets.

Playtime

Rabbits kept in the house or outside should be given the chance to behave naturally. In the wild, a rabbit would dig burrows and forage for food. Rabbits must eat plenty of grass or hay to keep their teeth and digestive system in good order.

All rabbits, should be given toys to play with, lots of hay, and you may even wish to teach them tricks.

Teaching tricks can be a great way of bonding with your rabbits and is lots of fun (see Orr and Lewin in further reading).

You can help your rabbits to live a full life by doing the following:

- Give your rabbits plenty of hay every day.

- Toys made of natural, untreated wood, such as willow are ideal.

- Do not give hard plastic toys, they will lead to potential teeth problems and if a rabbit swallows a fragment it may become extremely ill.

- Make a dig box, which is a cardboard box filled with hay. You can scatter this with some fresh herbs, or pelleted rabbit food. This gives your rabbits the chance to dig among the hay.

- Fill a dog activity ball with the rabbit's daily ration of pelleted food. Your rabbits will learn to roll it along to release the treats.

Where do I get my rabbits from?

There will be a wide variety of rabbits available at your local pet store, kept in spacious runs so you will have the opportunity to watch them and make your choice.

You could consider giving unwanted rabbits a new home. Many pet stores now have adoption centres and of course there are many associations that are constantly looking to re-home unwanted pets.

If you are interested in a particular breed, then you may wish to get your rabbits from a reputable breeder.

Signs of a healthy rabbit

Check that the rabbit you choose is fit and well.

Mouth

There should be no signs of dribbling, which could mean the teeth are overgrown.

Eyes

Look for bright, clear eyes, with no discharge.

Ears

Check the inside of the ears to see if they are clean. There should be no sign of damage on the outer ear.

Coat

The coat should be clean and glossy, with no scurf or bald patches.

Body

The body should be well covered, with no lumps or swellings.

Tail

Check under the tail for any matting or soiling, which could indicate diarrhoea, and is a sign that your rabbit may have teeth or intestine problems.

Breathing

Get close to the rabbit to check its breathing, which should be quiet and regular.

Movement

Look for the typical bunny hop; there should be no sign of lameness.

Making friends

If you spend time getting to know your rabbits, they will stop being frightened of you and become very tame. When you first bring your rabbits home, you will be desperate to stroke and play with them, but you must be patient. For the first couple of days, your rabbits need peace and quiet to get used to their new home. You will need to provide food, and change the water, so your rabbits will start getting used to you, without the stress of being handled.

Handling

When your rabbits appear to be happy and relaxed, you can start making friends.

- To begin with, come close to the hutch or cage, and talk to your rabbit. Do not make any sudden movements which will alarm it.

- Offer a treat so the rabbit has to come up to see you, and gets used to your hand.

- Now try stroking your rabbit, briefly just before you give it a treat. Most rabbits love to have their foreheads scratched, and will learn to sit perfectly still.

The next stage is to get the rabbit out of the hutch or cage. Be very careful, as a rabbit is quite heavy, and will panic easily. Rabbit do not like being carried around, and find it very scary. As soon as the rabbit is out of the hutch, settle it on the floor or on the ground. When your rabbit becomes tamer, try holding it on your lap. This process is much easier if the rabbit can access the run itself from the hutch as it means you will not be scaring it as you try to catch and carry it from the hutch to the run.

If your rabbit needs to be picked up, place one hand underneath the chest and the other around its hindquarters. Using the hand underneath the rabbit, lift upwards and use your other hand to support the weight. A rabbit should NEVER be picked up by its ears.

Do not turn your rabbit on its back and stroke its tummy. It will lie very still, because this is a scary position for rabbits – they are playing dead. It may also suddenly kick out to 'escape' and you may get injured.

Other pets

If you have other pets, such as a dog or cat or ferret you will need to be very careful, especially if you are keeping house rabbits or allow your rabbits free access to areas where other pets are around.

To start with, the dog should meet the rabbits when they are safely in the hutch or cage. The rabbits will feel frightened, so keep the dog at a distance. Reward the dog with a tasty treat if it remains calm and well behaved.

Repeat this exercise many times until the dog loses interest in the rabbits. But, remember, you should never allow other pets near the rabbits without supervision. Dog, cats and ferrets are meat-eaters and rabbit is one of their natural foods.

Food glorious food

A well-balanced diet will keep your rabbit happy and healthy, and will help to ensure a good, long life.

In the wild, rabbits eat grass and plants. It is essential that rabbits eat a lot of grass shaped food, which contains high fibre - such as hay. This stops their teeth growing too long, and ensures their guts work. If not they can quickly suffer from gut stasis and die or suffer serious and painful dental problems.

It is very important not to over-feed, particularly if you have house rabbits. Rabbits living in a hutch need more food to give them the energy to stay warm. House rabbits do not need to do this, and will easily become overweight.

Rabbits need a high level of fibre in their diet, and this is supplied by eating hay or grass. Dried grass is available, but hay is usually easier to obtain. Make sure you buy good-quality hay that smells sweet. Do not feed hay that is dusty or mouldy.

Hay should be available to your rabbits at all times, and should be the main part of their diet.

Vegetables

Rabbits love fresh vegetables. The best plan is to introduce one vegetable at a time so that your rabbits can get used to it.

Rabbit favourites include clover and sorrel, dandelion leaves, spinach and watercress. They also enjoy carrots (sliced into strips), celery, sweetcorn and broccoli.

Some leafy vegetables should be offered with caution as they can cause digestive problems such as bloat or diarrhoea.

These include cabbage (can cause bloat in young rabbits) and cauliflower (the leaf only, not the head). Other leafy greens can be offered in small quantities. If large amounts are given, especially if the rabbit is not used to fresh greens, these can trigger serious digestive upsets and diarrhoea. Avoid salad vegetables such as tomatoes, lettuce and cucumber which, although much enjoyed, have no beneficial properties and can cause diarrhoea.

When giving any fresh food to your pet it is important to make sure it is rinsed well under cold water to clean away any dirt or insects. You should never feed any fruit or vegetable that is over or under-ripe or that is wilting, as this is not healthy for your rabbits.

A good rule of thumb to follow is: would you eat it? If not then do not feed it to your pet.

Never collect fresh plants from the side of the road or from areas that have been, or are likely to have been, sprayed with pesticides as this is harmful to your rabbits. Instead, try to grow your own fresh herbs and vegetables for your pets. Not only will they taste fresh and crisp but it will also be great fun for your children or yourself to grow the treats.

Complete diet

There are a number of diets that are specially made for rabbits, which contain the nutrients needed to keep your rabbit healthy. Because rabbits are naturally 'fussy' eaters, known as selective feeders, pelleted diets are better than muesli type. However, whichever type you choose, these should not form the bulk of your rabbits' diet. Overfeeding of such diets can lead to problems with the rabbits' teeth and intestines, obesity, flystrike, boredom and aggression. As a rough guide, 25 g of a complete pelleted diet per kilo of bodyweight is appropriate. So if your rabbit weighs 3 kilos it should only have 75 g per day.

How much?

Rabbits are grazers, so they eat throughout the day and night. Hay should always be available for them. Vegetables and their ration of complete diet can be given once a day or split over two feeding times.

As a rough guide 70% of your rabbits' diet should be hay, 20% fresh vegetables and only 10% complete pellet or muesli type rabbit food.

Rabbit care

Looking after a rabbit means keeping its house clean and watching out for health problems. Cleaning out a cage or hutch might not be the most fun aspect of owning rabbits, but it is very rewarding when you think that you are making your rabbits as clean and comfortable as possible.

Daily tasks

Remove all uneaten food, and wash the feed bowls. If you frequently find uneaten food in the bowls, it means you are feeding too much–so give them less next time.

- Refill the water-bottle with fresh water.

- Refill the hayrack with fresh hay.

- Remove wet bedding and droppings (this is much easier if your rabbits use a litter tray).

- Give your rabbits access to the exercise run for several hours a day.

- Check your rabbit's bottom to ensure it is clean.

See 'Health' on page 112 for more information on daily checks.

Weekly tasks

Confine your rabbits to the exercise area so you can clean the cage or hutch thoroughly.

- Remove all bedding and clean out the cage or hutch with an 'animal friendly' disinfectant.

- If your rabbits use a litter tray, remove all litter, clean the tray, and replace with clean litter.

- Clean the water bottle.

- Replace all bedding material.

- Check your rabbits' teeth.

- Check your rabbits' nails.

- Groom your rabbits and check for mites or any other problems.

- Check your rabbits are not getting fat.

- Weigh your rabbits to check they are not losing or gaining weight.

Grooming

The amount of grooming each rabbit needs depends on coat length. All rabbits need brushing weekly, even short-haired ones.

However, long haired rabbits, such as Lionheads and Angoras, will need to be groomed every couple of days to prevent mats and tangles. Grooming helps keep the coat and underlying skin healthy. It also enables you to check for any problems.

Start grooming from an early age, perhaps when the rabbit is enjoying some tasty vegetables, so that it learns to relax and enjoy the attention.

Nails

In the wild, a rabbit would keep its nails in trim by digging. A pet rabbit's nails may grow too long, which will make moving very uncomfortable.

Nails can be clipped with nail-clippers used for dogs, but you will need to ask a vet or an experienced rabbit-keeper to do this for you, or show you how to do it.

Teeth

Keep a close check on your rabbit's teeth to make sure they do not grow too long. If your rabbit is drooling, or having difficulty eating, the teeth may need to be filed down or even removed. This is a job for the vet. Be warned, overgrown teeth can lead to serious and even fatal problems for rabbits. The chances of your rabbit developing problems is much less if they have lots of hay and vegetables to eat.

Rabbit behaviour

One of the most rewarding things about owning a pet is learning to understand what it is thinking or feeling.

If you have two or more rabbits, you will witness natural behaviour as the rabbits interact with each other. But you can also learn a lot about a single rabbit by listening to the sounds it makes, and observing its body postures.

Binky

This is an expression of pure joy. The rabbit jumps into the air, twisting its head and body in opposite directions.

Chin rubbing

Behaviour mostly seen in bucks. The rabbit is using scent glands under its chin to mark his territory/ property.

Crouching down

When a rabbit crouches, with ears flat and eyes bulging, it is telling you it is very frightened.

Lookout position

The rabbit is on its hind legs, with all senses on the alert, looking out for danger.

Lying stretched out

A relaxed, contented rabbit may lie on its side or tummy.

People greeting

A rabbit may 'greet' its owner by stretching its head towards you and flattening its ears. This is how it would greet another rabbit.

Tail bolt upright

A doe will do this when she is ready for mating.

Tail held out, ears flat

An angry or frightened rabbit.

Spitting

A sign of aggression, from a frightened or angry rabbit.

Thumping the ground with hindlegs

This is an alarm signal, used to warn other rabbits of danger.

Listen to your rabbit

Rabbits often grind their teeth. A rapid, gentle grinding sound means your rabbit is content; a slow, harsh, grinding sound means the rabbit is in pain.

Cooing

A doe may coo to her young, or rabbits may coo to each other if they are relaxed and secure.

Growling

A noise made by an angry rabbit.

Screaming

Hopefully you will never hear this. It is a shriek made by an extremely terrified rabbit.

Health

Rabbits can live up to 10–12 years, but sadly the majority live only 4 to 6 years. This short life is usually due to owners not understanding the rabbits' needs and providing a poor diet and inadequate accommodation.

Handling your pet every day and performing regular health checks will help you pick up on the early signs of ill health and take action quickly to treat ailments before they become too serious. This is best done while handling your pet in the normal way. You should do any examinations as part of your grooming and regular play.

Weigh your rabbits on a regular basis and remember to keep a record of their weight. Weight loss is often the first sign of ill health in rabbits.

You should know how your pet behaves while healthy. A sudden change in their normal pattern can also indicate ill health, such as change in their eating habits, hiding more or becoming aggressive.

Rabbits are prey animals and so are very good at disguising signs of illness, so familiarity with your own pets is vital. As a guide, signs of a poorly rabbit can include a thickly greasy coat, hunched body, faded and dull eyes and loose stools. They may press their stomach hard against the floor or roll to the side, or you may see panting while your rabbit is looking distressed. It is important that you contact a vet as soon as possible if you have any concerns about your rabbit's health.

Vaccinations

Rabbits can be vaccinated against two serious infections – Myxomatosis and Viral Haemorrhagic Disease (VHD/ RHVD/ RCD). These diseases can be fatal and vaccination offers the best possible chance of immunity. Even rabbits kept indoors are at risk and should be vaccinated.

Myxomatosis vaccination needs to be repeated every 6 months, and VHD once a year. Consult your vet for advice.

The sick bed

It is prudent to have a spare cage available if you have a sick rabbit. Keep them in sight of their cage friend to prevent stress unless you are told otherwise by your vet.

If you think your rabbit is unwell, you must seek veterinary help. Signs such as diarrhoea, or a swollen tummy or a lack of interest in food, can all indicate problems that can quickly become fatal, even within a day. It is important to seek veterinary help as early as possible.

Take you rabbit to the vet in a secure box, a cat carrying box is ideal.

Illness & injuries

Accidents, injuries or illness are inevitable throughout the years your rabbit is in your care. In the first instance a vet should be contacted to arrange treatment. But, in the time between the discovery of a problem and reaching the vet surgery you are in charge of providing the best care you can.

Mishaps

Because rabbits are so easily frightened they may be dropped or hurt when trying to run away from something that has scared them. They have very fine bones which can easily fracture. If you believe your pet has suffered a broken or fractured bone, phone your vet immediately. Your vet may advise you to bring your rabbit in as soon as possible for stabilization and pain relief.

Take your rabbit to the vet in a box lined with some soft bedding, and in the meantime keep it in a darkened and quiet area. It will feel more safe and relaxed in a dark enclosed space, a cat carrying box is ideal.

Wounds

Injuries to paws and eyes are very common in rabbits, often through hay seed or hay strands becoming lodged in their feet or tear ducts. Bites from cage mates also occur especially on the ears or nose. These injuries indicate all is not well between your rabbits and that they may not have enough space or things to do. You should seek behaviour advice from your vet.

Most minor injuries can be treated at home with a salt wash solution and a cotton pad, but more serious injuries must be looked at and treated by a veterinary surgeon as soon as possible to prevent infection.

Try to keep the wounded area as clean as possible until you can see a vet. The best way to do this is to prepare a solution of rock salt and warm water. If at all possible, cover the wound after washing to prevent any further risk of infection entering the wound until you can visit your veterinary practitioner.

Constipation & diarrhoea

These conditions should be taken very seriously as they can have a number of causes and can rapidly be fatal. Both can be caused by a poor diet or an illness. Consult a vet for advice and treatment.

Parasites

Scratching is a common symptom of a skin complaint often brought about by parasites such as lice, mites and fleas. Rabbits are usually free from parasites but should your pet get an infestation, treatment may involve a specialised medicated shampoo, mild insecticide powder or small animal spot-on preparation. Do not use treatments designed for dogs and cats as these can be fatal to rabbits. If you have any queries, seek veterinary advice. The most common parasite is the fur mite Chyletiella. This causes scruffy, flaky patches of dandruff-like skin. Look really closely and you may see the mites move, hence its alternative name of wandering dandruff.

Respiratory infections

Rabbits commonly carry bacteria which can cause lung disease, and an upper respiratory tract condition called 'snuffles' is also seen.

These infections if left untreated can lead to pneumonia. Avoid a damp environment and, if the symptoms continue, consult your veterinarian for further advice. Note that rabbits with a pale discharge from their eyes frequently have underlying dental disease. This can be avoided by feeding a correct diet.

Bloat

Bloat occurs when there is a build up of gas in the stomach and the bowel, typically the caecum. It can be caused by a wide variety of problems including stress, secondary infections, liver coccidiosis, and foreign bodies or, as is often the case, a sudden change in diet. The most obvious signs of bloat are a swollen hard stomach, lack of appetite, lethargy and dehydration. Veterinary advice should be sought as soon as possible if you suspect bloat as it can be fatal. A similar condition called mucoid enteropathy is seen in rabbits younger than 12–16 weeks of age.

Eye injuries

These are very common in rabbits and are often caused by hay or straw poking into their eyes. A saline wash to flush the eye and release any foreign bodies is worthwhile. You should contact your veterinary surgeon at once if the eye is held closed or appears opaque. The eyesight, or the eye itself may be lost if treatment is delayed.

Teeth

Dental disease is common in all rabbits and in dwarf and lop breeds in particular. Dental problems that occur in young rabbits less than four months old, are likely to be congenital, that is to say that it is just the way that rabbit is put together. Incisor tooth malocclusions are a typical example. Either the upper or lower incisor teeth fail to meet and wear against their opposite number, allowing them to overgrow. Incisor extraction by your vet may solve this problem. In older rabbits the problem is likely to be acquired dental disease and this is usually linked to poor diet, in particular a lack of hay leading to inadequate wear of the cheek teeth. In the worst cases tooth root abscesses can develop and the condition can become intractable.

Long term treatment, with repeated anaesthetics to treat the teeth, may be required. Even then, secondary abscesses and bone infection may result. Many rabbits with advanced dental disease are put to sleep.

Fly strike

Normally a problem in the summer months, it is caused by the blow flies laying eggs in faeces-soiled fur around the hind end of your rabbit. These hatch within 24 hours and eat their way into the skin around the rabbit's rectum. You should check your pet on a daily basis to ensure their bottoms are free from faeces. If your rabbit does have a bottom with faeces stuck to it this could indicate teeth problems, digestive problems or that your rabbit is too fat. In these circumstances you should see your vet.

There are treatments which can help prevent flies being around the cage/hutch, but these are not 100% effective, so you must check your rabbit daily.

If you see fly eggs or maggots, this is a veterinary emergency and you should contact your vet if you think your rabbit may have been attacked. Delay can result in your rabbit being literally eaten alive by maggots.

Worms

Worms are rare in pet rabbits although roundworms and tapeworms are occasionally a problem. Symptoms include a distended abdomen, poor coat, a crouching posture and (rarely) worms in the faeces. Occasionally cyst-like intermediate forms of tapeworms may develop in rabbits exposed to grass soiled by unwormed dogs. These form fluid filled swelling under the skin or deeper in the body.

Rabbit medicine

Veterinary knowledge of rabbits has increased hugely over the last few years and there is now much more that can be done for your pet. However, unlike cat and dog medicine which all veterinary surgeons know a lot about, rabbits like other small animals, are somewhat of a specialist subject, and it is worth finding a vet who is interested in rabbits and their treatment.

Know your
pet rabbit

Scientific name	Oryctolagus cuniculus
Group order	Lagomorpha
Female breeding period	Induced ovulation
Gestation	30- 33 days from successful mating
Litter size	4- 6 (average)
Birth weight	40- 100 g approx
Birth type	Naked, blind, dependent
Eyes open	10- 12 days approx
Weaning	5- 6 weeks
Breeding age	
Doe	4- 5 months; from 6 months optimum
Buck	3- 4 months

Further reading

McBride, E.A. 1988 Rabbits and Hares. Whittet Books.

McBride, A. 2000 2nd Edition Why Does My Rabbit....?
Souvenir Press
Magnus, E 2002 How To Have A Relaxed Rabbit.
UK Pet Behaviour Centre.

Moore, L.C. 2005 A House Rabbit Primer. Santa Monica Press.

Orr, J and Lewin, T 2005 Getting Started: Clicking With Your
Rabbit. Karen Pryor Publications.

Richardson, V 1999 Rabbit Nutrition. Coney Publications.
An illustrated guide to plants and vegetables, wild and
cultivated that can be fed to your rabbit.

Websites

www.rabbitwelfare.co.uk – the rabbit welfare association
provides lots of useful information on rabbits and veterinary
surgeons around the UK who have a special interest in
treating rabbits.

www.rabbit.org – website of the House Rabbit Society of the
USA

http://wales.gov.uk/docs/drah/
publications/091109rabbitsumen.pdf - How to look after your
rabbit – following the code. A booklet produced by the Welsh
government giving advice on your legal responsibilities to
your rabbit under the UK Animal Welfare Act (2006).

Weights & measures

If you prefer your units in pounds and inches, you can use this conversion chart:

Length in inches	Length in cm	Weight in kg	Weight in lb
1	2.5	0.5	1.1
2	5.1	0.7	1.5
3	7.6	1	2.2
4	10.2	1.5	3.3
5	12.7	2	4.4
8	20.3	3	6.6
10	25.4	4	8.8
15	38.1	5	11

Measurements rounded to 1 decimal place.